I0172895

Divine Assignment

Living My Life with

Purpose

Written by

Sheri Simmons

Printed in the United States of America

First Printing, 2019

ISBN Number 9780985319977

―――――――――――――――――――――――

"And you shall know the truth, and the truth shall make you free."

John 8:32 NKJ

If you are looking for a road map to finding your purpose, this book is for you. Each of us has been given a divine assignment. It's up to us to find out what that undertaking is. If you are seeking peace and clarity in your life, I urge you to read this rendition of how one person's experience can change a generation. I found this book to be transparent to the point of pain. The writer had the courage to share her truth. This book grants a pathway and plan to better guide your own toils and snares. It is not only autobiographical, but it is also devotional. A thought provoking and insightful take on life's journey. The author allows you the freedom to map out your individual assignment with a thought-provoking method of soul searching. Whatever you are going through or have been through remember, you are living your life FOR A DIVINE

PURPOSE.   When you know the truth, you will surely be FREE.

Reverend Rozetta Jackson

Doctor of Ministry

Senior Pastor and Organizer

Cities of Refuge Ministries Incorporated

Mount Vernon, New York

Acknowledgements

Giving all honor to God who is the head of my life. I am truly blessed to be able to even write this book. I have been on a journey of transformation for many years. The person that I am today had to go through things that would have killed the average person. I know that I am not average. I know that I was put here to do something big. And that is exactly what I am going to do. I am living a very full and purposeful life. This life I live means so much more because of my passion and purpose.

I want to first thank all the people who have doubted me, lied on me, called me out of my name and tried to destroy my character. In any other circumstance I wouldn't acknowledge any of you. However, you are a great part of this is story. Because of you I am so much stronger and wiser. Thanks for the lessons that you have taught me. I needed to know that everyone doesn't have great intentions. I needed to understand that everyone is not my friend. It's all good, I have forgiven and moved on from everything that was meant to break me. I had to because *Romans 12:19* says *Dearly Beloved, avenge not yourselves, but rather give place unto wrath: for it is written, Vengeance is mine, I will repay, saith the Lord.*

To the wonderful people who started on this journey with me or   joined along the way, I thank you. There are so many of you to thank. Please don't blame my heart if you aren't listed. Know that I   appreciate each one of you.

To my best friend and right-hand Thelma Brown. We have been through so much in life and we are still together. I wouldn't change any minute of our time as friends. Thank you for always having my back. Thank you for helping me with my children. And most of all thank you and your family for inviting me into your lives and home.

To my dear husband Jason Simmons. Life got better when you came around. You give me strength and confidence to achieve any goal I set. You even push me to achieve what I think is the impossible. Thank you for putting up with me flaws and all. It takes a strong man to love a broken woman. I am a work in progress, and I appreciate having your love and support.

To the three-little people in my life, Jaylin, Jayson and Jayshaun. I love you guys to pieces. You each came at a different point in my life and changed it for the better. Being your mom is the greatest title I could ever have. I want you boys to be and do better than me. I grind hard because I want you to work smarter and not harder.

To my new friends who came in my life. Mayia, Shamen, Jermiel, Jimmy, Nancy, Rocio, Evonne, Lisaret, and Jeannette. Thank you, guys, for your encouraging words, your support, and being genuine. I look forward too many more years as friends as all of us accomplish our individual goals.

Note from the Author

I am using the Good News Bible Translation. I wanted anyone who picks this book up to be able to understand the bible verses.

Dedication

This book is dedicated to my first-born son Jaylin. I am very proud to be your mom.

What is my purpose?

Jeremiah 29:11 For I know the plans I have for you." declares the Lord, "plans to prosper you and not to harm you, plans to give you hope and a future.

I was asked to be on a panel for a women's empowerment event that was held in October 2018. The theme was Seeking True Purpose. I was asked to answer the following questions.

1. What is your purpose?

2. How did you find your purpose?

3. When you found your purpose, how did you move differently in life?

The questions weren't hard to answer at all. I had fifteen minutes to answer the three questions. I knew for a while before the event what my purpose was. The issue was that my purpose wasn't specific enough and so I had to do some digging. I was asked to speak at this event in August. The event was in October. I had a little over 5 weeks to find the answer suitable for a crowd of 50+ women. I wasn't the only speaker. I was one of five. At the time of the invite, I didn't know which order I was in. I suppose it really didn't matter at the time. But when the event came near, I was asked to go first. I wasn't confident when I said yes. So, I dig even deeper to give a speech that packed a powerful punch.

Things happen for a reason they say. Yes, this statement is so true. The month before I was invited to speak, I spent a few days in San Jose California. My friend Mayia was reading a book called Believe Bigger: Discover the Path to Your Life Purpose by Marshawn Evens Daniel. All I saw was the cover and I knew I needed to read it. I never was a fan of self-help books. I didn't know that this was a spiritual self-help book. Now these are my favorite things to read. When I got home, I started reading it. When I was asked to do the purpose speech, I couldn't believe what was happening. I love reading but I don't get to read as often as I like. I based my speech on the Believe Bigger book. She talks about how passion comes from disruption. I sure knew what she was talking about when I read it. My life was disrupted quite a few times from being in a domestic violence relationship, to having my first child, to getting a divorce. . Some things were for the best, I know that now.

So, what is my purpose? Often, we confuse purpose with gifts and talents. I knew I wanted to help people since I was five years old. At five I told my mama I wanted to be a doctor. When I realized that I need to be good in math and science was the day that dream died. But I still had it in me to help people. I was so busy looking for a job to help people, that I had no idea I was helping people with my words and stories. As I dug deeper into my passion, gifts and talents, I came up with this opening sentence to my speech. "My purpose is to help people. More specifically to led, encourage, educate, inspire, influence, and motivate."

I am a very gifted and talented writer. I know that but I never wanted to share my work. I am a private person. I kept a lot of journals. Writing was and still is therapeutic for me. Storytelling was natural for me. People told me all the time I should be an author or comedian. I chose the author route. I feel that I don't say things to be funny, it comes out that way but that's not my intention. Back then I suffered from low self-esteem. I know now to be a great writer you need to be confident. No confidence, then your book is not going to survive. I decided in 2011 to give book writing a try. I didn't have a clue what I was doing but I was going to figure it out. One thing about me is that I am very resourceful. If I don't know something I'm going to research and find a way to get started.

As a kid, I was very shy. I didn't like to talk to people. I think it came from my mom overloading me with activities. I was in Girl Scouts, Dance, Cadets, etc. It was overwhelming at the time. But I thank her for the overload. Now I join groups and events all the time to network and collaborate with people.

As I got older, I became very reserved and observant with people. People started labeling me anti-social. The idea of public speaking scared me back then. But now I love it. Give me a microphone and I feel like I'm in a whole different world. A world where nothing matters but me and my words. To get to this point I had to develop thick skin and self-confidence. Wasn't easy but I did it. In a way I had no choice. It was either stop speaking because people complained about my voice, or they didn't condone what I spoke about, or do what I loved and forget what everyone was saying. You know already know which option I chose.

So back to my purpose. Through the words I speak and write I am able to   lead, encourage, educate, inspire, influence, and motivate. I didn't know that I could have such powerful things to say and write. But that's not me. It's no one but God. God gave me the gift of speaking and writing. The gifts aren't for me though. They are to be shared with any and everyone who may need to read my books or hear my voice. I have these gifts and I am grateful for them. I must use them, or they will be taken away. What better way to use them than in my purpose?

Often people confuse the definition of gifts and talents. To me they aren't the same. A person could be talented but not gifted. A person could be gifted and not talented or gifted and talented. Gifts are given to   us from God. Talents are things that we become skilled to do. Gifts are part of your calling. Because people confuse these terms, is the reason many are walking around lost. I have spoken to some many women about purpose. And the first thing I ask is what's your passion. Some can't answer the question. Passion indicates purpose but it's more than that. If you know what you're passionate about then you can   narrow down finding what your purpose is.

The person I am today can't imagine walking around lost without knowing what my passion is. I understand because I used to be in their shoes. It is very painful walking around lost in world of people. There are many people just existing in life and not living it. But I was able to go through the pain and still figure it out. How did I do it? The next chapters will detail all the heartache, pain and misery I went through to get to become who I am today. My journey is not for the faint of heart. I speak my truth because I want to help others get through their issues. Issues that I have dealt with. Issues that have plagued my mind and spirit. So now I ask you.

Do you know what your purpose

is?_____

_____

_____

If you do what is it?

_____

_____

_____

If you don't, do you know what your passion

is?_____

_____

_____

If you can't answer any of the above question do not worry. Use the next couple of pages to do some soul searching on your purpose and passion.

_____

_____

_____

_____

_____

_____

_____

_____

_____

_____

_____

_____

_____

_____

_____

_____

Divine Assignment

_____

_____

_____

_____

_____

_____

_____

_____

_____

_____

_____

_____

_____

_____

_____

_____

_____

_____

_____

_____

_____

_____

_____

_____

Divine Assignment

When God calls, You better answer

Romans 8:28 And we know that in all things God works for the good of those who love him, who have been called according to his purpose.

I suffer from depression and PTSD. I found that out in 2013. Prior to 2013, I was walking around broken and hurt. Trying to please everyone around me. But doing that only lead to misery and pain. After a while I had no idea who I was. I didn't know what I liked, I didn't know anything about myself. I was always attempting to make everyone else happy that I stayed sad. I allowed people to disrespect me and tear away at my dignity. There were days that I felt lower than the ground. How does someone pick themselves up after years of feeling tormented and abused? For me I was sick and tired of being sick and tired.

I was depressed as a teenager. I didn't know it at the time. I thought about cutting my wrist many days just to get away from my home life. I never did it, but that's how bad I wanted to leave home. I felt like I was the mom of my three siblings. I felt that I should have been living a teenage life. Instead I was home all the time with my siblings. I was held accountable for their actions. It was nerve wrecking and unbearable. It even got to the point where I decided at a young age that I did not want to have children. I have three wonderful children now. Never say never!

When I graduated from high school, I was so happy. Not because I finally was done with school. But because I was able to make my own decisions. My 18th birthday was a month after graduation. The first decision that I made on my own was to leave my mother's house. I knew there was a world out there for me to see. I knew that if I stayed, I would never see the world the way I wanted.

Sometimes we live our lives according to other people's wants and needs for us. That's what I did when I enrolled in college right after high school. I wanted to get a job and travel, but my family wanted me to go to school. So, I did. And I was miserable. Misery loves company they say. They were so right. I ended up getting expelled from school. I was glad that I didn't have to go back to school anymore. But I was disappointed that I hurt my grandmother. She was my biggest supporter up until the day she passed away. So, I decided to right my wrong and enroll in school. Again, not doing something for me but for someone else. The good news is I got ended up graduating with an associate degree. The bad news is sixteen years later the degree is collecting dust. I never used it or the other degree once. That is another story to be told.

In the first school I attended I failed Introduction to writing class. I knew that   wasn't correct. I loved writing. I was better at writing then verbal communications. I was always being told I should publish my work. I was always being praised for what a good writer I was. So, to see on paper that I was a failure hurt. That F is on my transcript forever. I just knew that I was a good writer. When people aren't told what they want to hear they usually stay quit. They usually throw all their hard work away. What if I had taken that grade of F to heart and stopped writing. You wouldn't be reading this book. What if Taraji P Henson didn't move to California because she was told she was too old. We wouldn't have one of the fiercest black stars in Hollywood. My point is that we are going to fail at things. Even things that we are good at. But that doesn't mean that we should quit the things that we are passionate about. There are some things I love but do not love doing. I love having my hair and nails done. I don't like doing my own hair and nails. It's ok to quit something that you tried and don't like. It doesn't make you a failure. I used to think that it did. I think the failure comes from never making the attempt to do something. How does one know what they are good at if they don't try? Fear is a powerful thing. Fear causes people not to do what they want or need to do. There are a couple of acronyms regarding the word FEAR. The one that I want to talk about is False Evidence Appearing Real.   Have you ever heard someone say they were afraid to succeed? I have heard it countless times. I think people who say this are crazy. What's the point of venturing out and going into a business? What's the point of spending money to get degrees of success is not part of the equation? Fear paralyzes people to the point that they forget their hopes and dreams. God has a plan for you and me. It doesn't matter what you want to do, if you are called his will be done. I never wanted to be an author. My writing was private. As I wrote my stories, I realized that I was inspiring and teaching people through my words. My message was needed to be heard. If you have a passion get to work and use your gifts to make something happen. Once God calls you, you can't ignore the call no matter how hard you try. You might as well suck it up and answer. You can start getting to your calling by answering these questions.

Do you know

calling?_____

_____

_____

    Have you missed opportunities because you felt like you

weren't

ready?_____

_____

_____

    What is holding you back from achieving your

dreams?_____

_____

_____

    Be honest with yourself. Your answers are not for me. They are to help you get to where you want to be. You can't there with no clarity. You won't get there lying to yourself. If you can't answer the questions, use the next couple of pages to do some more soul searching.

_____

_____

_____

_____

Divine Assignment

Divine Assignment

_____

_____

_____

_____

_____

_____

_____

_____

_____

_____

_____

_____

_____

_____

_____

_____

_____

_____

_____

_____

_____

_____

_____

Divine Assignment

Galatians 1:15 But God in his grace chose me even before I was born and called me to serve.

I'm not supposed to be alive. When I was born, I had breathing and heart problems. My sister who was born a couple of minutes before me was born stillborn. The doctor told my mom I wasn't going to be smart. And as I progressed in my childhood, I suffered from asthma and scoliosis. But God kept me and held me close. He knew that what He wanted me to do in life.

I almost died at the hands of an ex-boyfriend in 2006. The brutal attack left me with fractured ribs and a scar on my right arm from him cutting me with a knife. I literally saw my life flash before my eyes. I felt that in that moment I was going to die. Yet thirteen years later, I am still here. The scripture says it all. God calls who he wants for the purpose he needs. I feel that I am not qualified for the call, but He does. So, what I feel doesn't matter.   I just do what is required to satisfy the call.

As I get older, the call is easy. But in my teens and young adulthood it was so difficult. I was struggling to figure out who I was. Since I didn't have proper guidance from my parents growing up, everything I learned was through experience. My father wasn't around, and my mom was emotionally not there. Some of the things I experienced, I wouldn't wish on my worst enemy. I cried, I got my heart broken, I was lied to. But it's ok now. At the time it wasn't funny and hurt so bad. I can look back now and see every heartache as a lesson.

I named this book Divine Assignment after I went to a women auxiliary weekend at a church. This was my first-time attending church three days in a row. I was so used to going to church Sundays and occasionally Saturdays. I had never seen this particular pastor who preached on that particular day. She kept saying " You are not here by accident, but by Divine Assignment." She went on to say that things that we go through aren't for us. They are for us to share with others. Testimonies help other people. That is one of the ways that God uses people. I took that to mean that everything I have been through wasn't an accident. The awful things that I endured should be shared with people to help them overcome their troubles. It's amazing how God turns messes into messages!

Speaking about the troublesome events in my life has been very therapeutic. I have done countless speaking engagements. I love being able to connect with others. I love when people say that they were moved by my story. I feel that I am speaking for those with no voice. It makes me very sad to know that many people are working around lost with no one to talk to. I wish that I could just hug them all and let them know it is going to be ok. That despite what they are going through or have gone through, God has their back. I don't believe in dwelling on the past. Why? Because it happened already. What can I do about it? I want people to understand that I am not what I have been through. I forgive, learned and moved on. Forgiveness is for us not the other person. The Bible says in *Luke 17:3-4* "*So watch what you do. If your brother sins, rebuke him, and if he repents, forgive. If he sins against you seven times in one day, and each time he comes to you saying, "I repent", you must forgive him.*" To me forgiveness has a few grey areas. Are we to keep forgiving and giving people chances to hurt us? I say no. For me the first time I forgive and do not allow the same person to fool me again. We can't go on a diving assignment if we can't do what the bible says. Yes, some of the things are hard to do. We are human. We have emotions and have the right to feel what we feel. But we need to find a balance between the Word of God and our human emotions. Easier said than done, I know. But it can be done. And trust me you will feel so much better when you follow the word of God instead of Man.

So, what is your Divine Assignment?

_____

_____

_____

Were you afraid of your assignment?_____

_____

_____

_____

How do you feel about your assignment?_____

_____

_____

I know it may seem scary answering these questions. Your friends and family may not ever ask you these questions. But these questions are so important in figuring out your purpose. Take some time and jot down whatever comes to mind.

_____

_____

_____

_____

_____

_____

_____

_____

_____

_____

_____

_____

_____

_____

_____

_____

Divine Assignment

_____

_____

_____

_____

_____

_____

_____

_____

_____

_____

_____

_____

_____

_____

_____

_____

_____

_____

_____

_____

_____

_____

_____

Divine Assignment

_____

_____

_____

_____

_____

_____

_____

_____

_____

_____

_____

_____

_____

_____

_____

_____

_____

_____

_____

_____

_____

_____

_____

Dealing with Depression

Psalm 23- The Lord is my shepherd; I have everything I need. 2. He lets me rest in fields of green grass and leads me to quiet pools of fresh water. 3.He gives me new strength. He guides me in the right paths, as he has promised. 4. Even if I go through the deepest darkness, I will not be afraid, Lord, for you are with me. Your shepherd's rod and staff protect me. 5. You prepare a banquet for me, where all my enemies can see me; you welcome me as an honored guest and fill my cup to the brim. 6. I know that your goodness and love will be with me all my life; and your house will be my home as long as I live.

Depression is real. The sad part about it is that mental health is just now being recognized as a problem. If mental health was a priority and made important years ago, think of all the people who could benefit. I can't even place the blame on the medical profession, or the government. In the black community it's shunned upon to speak about therapy and medicine. I couldn't express my feelings of sadness and despair around my family. Therapy was frowned upon. So of course, I ended up in a very severe situation twice. The outcome was better than what could have happen. But still if

I had known that I was depressed I wouldn't have chosen to do what I did. I would have sought out other alternatives.

In 2007, I felt like my life was overloaded. I was still feeling the effects of coming out of a domestic violence situation. I am going to speak more about it in a later chapter. In dealing with this situation, I never sought help. I spoke about it to someone at a crisis center, but she made me feel like crap. I don't like being interrogated. She made me feel like I deserved what happened to me. She was very forceful in telling me if I wanted help, I needed to speak to law enforcement. I don't mind answering questions. I didn't appreciate feeling like I did something wrong. Furthermore, I just wasn't ready to report what was done to me. I feel that I am the most authentic and transparent person anyone can ever know. However, I don't like when people try to make my issues and situations all my fault. I am aware of my part in each situation in my life. I also accept the part that I played.

Life suddenly became hard. I was overwhelmed. I was unhappy where I was staying. I felt like I was suffocating. So, I decided, while sitting up in my room. There was a window with an air conditioner inside of it. I opened the window and sat on top of the air conditioner. I sat on the edge and looked down. Being on the fifth floor, I knew it was a long drop down. All that was below me was a pile of garbage. If I decided to just drop, I doubt anyone would know what I had done for days. All that was on my mind was how to stop the feeling of being suffocation. I get what people who commit suicide are going through. When you have a bad feeling and it hurts so bad, you just want to stop it. It feels like so many emotions running through you at once. It hurts so bad physically and mentally. Sometimes unfortunately if no one is around suicide becomes the only way out. *Psalm 55:22 says "Leave your troubles with the Lord, and he will defend you; he never lets honest people be defeated."* Of course, I wasn't thinking about this.

Sitting outside the window was comforting. I started to feel much better. I knew I couldn't stay out there. I now had another decision to make. Go back inside or end it all. I choose to go back inside and find someone to talk to. My best friend Thelma wasn't around at the time. She is the one I talk to whenever I get in my depressive moments. But she wasn't there. So, I started researching suicide hotlines. I didn't want to speak to just anybody. My internet search was a complete bust. So, I called 311. 311 in NYC is an information call center. I asked the operator for a suicide hotline. In seconds the conversation went all the way to the left. I was asked all these questions as if I was doing something at the moment. I was completely thrown off when a 911 operator came on the phone line. I couldn't believe what was going on. The police showed up at my house, of course frightening my adoptive parents. I pleaded with the officer that I wasn't crazy and that I wasn't going to hurt myself. It didn't work. I ended up being taken to the hospital, placed in a strait jacket in room with padded walls. The bright lights were killing my eyes. I couldn't hardly move because of the weight of the jacket. I never in my life imagined that I would end up in a place like this. I wanted nothing more than to get out of there. The bible says in Psalm's the 56th chapter, verse 3 "When I am afraid, O Lord Almighty, I put my trust in you" I started to cry. The tears were coming from so many emotions at once. I was scared, I was tired, I was worried. Overall, I became exhausted and just wanted to go home.

When the door opened, it felt like a rush of fresh air came in. The cool air was heaven to my nostrils. A doctor came in with a few other medical people. The dreaded questions began. Questions such as "Do you want to harm yourself now?" How are you feeling now?" Who do you live with? Are you safe? I was more annoyed over the fact that I was still in the strait jacket. After the interrogation was over, I was told that I should do some outpatient therapy. I said ok but never did it. As I said before, therapy was frowned upon by everyone I was close too. However, I didn't want to suffer in silence anymore. I knew I needed to make some changes in my life. And so, I did. After I came home from the hospital I enrolled in college for Paralegal Studies. It was something new and different for me. I also started writing short stories. Writing was my therapy, and now I was writing stories about characters with real life details that were happening to me. It was the perfect way to get my pain out.

Thinking back to this incident, I was very lucky to not be committed. I just wish that I had taken the advice to go to therapy. Maybe if I had the next time, I ended up in the hospital for depression wouldn't have occurred. I wasn't so lucky the second time.

Have you or do you suffer with any mental illnesses?

_____

_____

Are you seeing a
professional?_____

_____

Currently I am in therapy and I have been for five years. It is nothing to be afraid or ashamed of. If you are having feelings and feel depressed, I urge you to seek help. Don't suffer in silence.

Major Break Down

Revelations 21:4 He will wipe all tears from your eyes. There will be no more death, no more grief or crying or pain. The old things have disappeared.

I said as a young adult that I never wanted to have children. The reason being came from me caring for my siblings as a kid and teenager. I didn't get to have a life or enjoy my childhood. I didn't want to be responsible for anyone but myself. I knew it was selfish of me. I thought I deserved to be selfish because of the many years I spent being a mom to my siblings. My selfish moment ended on November 5th, 2009. A couple of weeks before this date I was experiencing fatigue, and pain in my breast. I didn't pay it any mind cause at the time, I was in college with three jobs. Yes, three jobs. I liked nice things and I didn't have anyone to give me anything. I lived with my best friend and her family. They provided me with a roof over my head and food. I didn't want them to give me everything. I was raised by my grandmother who taught me, if I wanted something, I needed to work for it. And so that's what I did.

I ignored the symptoms until I missed my period. I was always on time. I knew my schedule like the back of my hand. I took a pregnancy test on Halloween and it was negative. I was so relieved, but I still was feeling tired. The following weekend I took another test. The two pink lines appearing made me scream in fear. I couldn't believe it. My friend said it was positive, I told her not the line was too light. She put it out the window to dry it and when she came back the lines were darker. Not wanting to believe that I was carrying a baby, I went to bed. I wanted to sleep and wake up as if this was a dream. Well that didn't happen. I was twenty-six years old having my first child. I was older than other girls I knew that I had kids. Most had their kids either as teens or early 20's. The only question I had was what do I do now?

Having a baby is very stressful in itself. To add to all the frustration, you have people who want to give their very irrelevant and unneeded opinions. Then you have all these different symptoms going on with your body. Being pregnant to me wasn't fun nor was it a happy time. Especially since I knew that I would be a single mom. I was ok with that even though I didn't want that for my son. I tried to go to work but I was so sick I had to take a leave until I had my son. I was so nauseous, I was in the ER nearly every other week.

Dealing with all these things was frustrating but what hurt me the most was the words that my grandmother said to me. " I am so disappointed in you" Her words broke me down and made me feel so low. All I wanted at that point was to go back to the way things were, before I became pregnant. Distressed and distraught I went to the hospital, to see what I could do. I wasn't thinking clearly. I was very upset and irrational. I learned that decision making in that state of mind is very dangerous. If I had known then what I knew now, I wouldn't have walked into the Emergency Room that day.

I was seen by a doctor who spoke to me for 2 minutes about how I was feeling. I was still distraught. I said I didn't want the baby. He left and came back saying he felt I was a danger to myself and the baby. What that meant was that I was committed against my will for 72 hours. Involuntary hospitalization is used to force mental ill patients to get treatment. The hospital I was in wasn't a mental health hospital. So, for two days I was stuck in the Emergency Room, while they searched for me a bed at another hospital.

The Emergency room is a zoo. When we are there as patients, we focus so much on our issues, we don't pay attention to everything that's happening.   I wasn't there being treated for anything. So, I was able to observe everything that was going on around me. People screaming about how long service was taking or because they are in so much pain, Nasty nurses being mean to patients, the fire department had to come and bring the jaws of life for a patient who had a ring on his penis. Some of the stuff I heard, and saw was comical. But I knew it wasn't funny for those who were going through it. I had someone watching me every second of the day. It was so annoying and frustrating. I had no one to talk to but the nurse who had to babysit me. I had a few kind ones and then a few mean ones. No one I knew came to see me. That was because all my stuff was taken from me and put away until I was able to get a room. So, for two days no one knew where I was.

The third day when I woke up in the ER, I was told I was moving to the maternity floor. I was excited to be getting out of the crazy emergency room. The way it's portrayed on tv is, the way I saw it. People constantly moving, talking and sometimes screaming. You would think overnight it would be less people but no not when I was there. People flood in and out of the Emergency room all day and all night.

Before I was taken upstairs, the nurse wanted to check the baby. She had the screen turned away from me as she looked. I was curious to see the baby. I hadn't seen him at all. At the time I was seven weeks. I looked over towards her. She asked me did I want to see. I said yes. She showed me the screen. She then said children are precious gifts from God. I knew then I couldn't terminate my pregnancy. I told her I wanted to speak to the doctor again. She said ok. I was taken to my room where I thought, things would be much better. But I was wrong.

When you stay in the hospital overnight or for a couple of days, you get three meals a day. But as a pregnant patient, I find that to be unacceptable. It baffled me that I had to argue with the nurses just to have a snack. Dinner is at 5 or 6 and I'm not expected to have anything until 7 the next morning. It wasn't like people were knocking on my door to visit me. I was truly alone. When I got transferred upstairs, I was given my phone. And I still had the nurse for observation. I was glad to be out of the E.R but now I felt like I was in prison. I couldn't use the bathroom without someone standing in front of the door. I even tried to stand outside my room door and the security guard told me to go back inside. I asked him where the hell was I going in a hospital gown. He looked at me like I was crazy and repeated "Go back in the room."

When the doctor came in to see me, he told me I was being transferred to another hospital later in the day. He said that it would be up to that doctor whether I got to go home. I don't like not being in control of decisions for myself. I cried like a baby. Of course, the doctor didn't care. He just walked out. There was nothing left for me to do but pray. Prayer is the key to everything. I must admit I don't pray as much as I should. I also must admit that I don't read my bible as much as I should. But in all the times of distress, I definitely prayed and read my bible. Hebrews 11:6 is one verse that I read over and over while in the hospital. The verse says, *"No one can please God without faith, for whoever comes to God must have faith that God exists and rewards those who seek him."* Having faith is so hard when you are in a dire situation and can't get yourself out. But I knew that things happen for a reason. I didn't know why I was going through, what I was going through. As I got older, I understood that the pain and heartache was for me to share with others. We go through things in life so we can be testimonies for other people. There are so many women that I had the opportunity to talk to and listen to their stories. They have no idea that I went through some rough things myself. You must go through things in order to lead, educate, motivate and inspire people. How can you help someone else when you don't understand where they are coming from and what they have been through?

When it came time for me to be transferred to the other hospital, I became violently ill. Of course, the doctor didn't want to treat me, he was more concerned with getting the bed ready for the next patient. Even though I wasn't feeling well to walk, I was on my way to another hospital bed. I kept saying I had to vomit. No one listened, so when I was placed in the ambulette, I let it out on the attendant. She wasn't mad at all. She said she never had anyone vomit on her before, but she was glad it was me. That made me laugh to see her humor in such a disgusting situation.

The rest of the night was spent in and out of the bathroom. I just felt so bad. My neighbor kept me up because she kept talking to herself. For my first time being in the psych ward, I never want to go back. People really do talk to themselves and see things that aren't there. It wasn't the place for me to be. I was just sad because I wasn't getting any type of support while pregnant. People were saying all sorts of mean and nasty things. I just couldn't deal with the cards that I was dealt.

Isaiah 40:29 "He strengthens those who are weak and tired." I am a   witness that God does just that. There was a light at the end of the tunnel for me. I met with the doctor in the morning. He said that I could go home under the condition that I went to outpatient therapy. I had to sign that I would go.   Having no choice, I agreed. I just wanted to go home. I was willing to see what therapy was all about. Nothing else really was working for me. People say go to church when you are depressed. I don't agree. The church is just the building. The people in it can be very mean and discouraging. I experienced people talking about me and starting rumors about me in the church. It's no surprise some people refuse to go to church. The church is supposed to be the place of spiritual healing and support. But I wasn't getting any of that. It made me realize that people who hold titles like Pastor, Preacher, Deacon, and Deaconess can be plain evil. They quickly use God's word to hurt people and then contradict the word with their behavior Monday through Saturday.

As I headed home from the hospital, I thanked God for a new beginning. I was going to be a mom and I needed all the strength and courage I could get to survive this pregnancy. *Philippians 4:13 I have the strength to face all conditions by the power that Christ gives me.*

Have you ever had a breakdown before?_____

_____

_____

How did you overcome it?_____

_____

_____

Were people around to help you through it?_____

_____

_____

What I have learned in therapy are coping mechanisms. You may realize that certain things or people trigger you to be sad. When we start to become aware of these things, we can make changes for our mental health's sake. Take some time and jot down some coping mechanisms that you can use when you feel like you are going to break down.

_____

_____

_____

_____

_____

_____

_____

_____

_____

_____

_____

_____

_____

_____

_____

_____

_____

_____

_____

_____

Divine Assignment

_____

_____

_____

_____

_____

_____

_____

_____

_____

_____

_____

_____

_____

_____

_____

_____

_____

_____

_____

_____

_____

_____

_____

_____

Being a first-time mom

Psalm 30:5 His anger lasts only a moment, his goodness for a lifetime. Tears may flow in the night, but joy comes in the morning.

My due date was July 8th, 2010. I was so happy because that was three weeks before my birthday July 29th. I was happy to have a baby for my birthday gift. However as most of us know, babies have their own timeline. Jaylin was born June 14th, 2010. It was the most stressful time of my life. I knew I needed to have a c-section. But knowing and then going through it are two different things. Prior to having Jaylin, I had a myomectomy in 2006. A myomectomy is a surgery to remove fibroids. It's like a c-section with the cut on the abdomen. Once someone has this surgery, any babies delivered must be via c-section.

I went to the hospital late at night around 11pm. I was in the most excruciating pain. When the doctor came to check me, she said she wanted to see if I had dilated any further. Weeks prior I had dilated to 1 cm. That required a week hospital stay and some medication to stop the contractions. At that time, I was only 33 weeks pregnant. This time I was 36 weeks pregnant. The closer you are to 37 weeks the better it is for baby.

After the doctor check me, she ran out of the room. I instantly knew something was wrong. The nurse entered the room and asked me was I ready to have a baby. I told her no. What kind of question is this to ask a first-time mom? I was alone. I didn't picture me being alone when I had to have a baby. She told me to call someone because the baby was going to come soon. I ended up calling his father. We weren't on the best terms, but he did want to be there for the birth of the baby.

The operating room is so cold. It's also busy. People moving around, talking, and instruments being shuffled about. I was laid on a table with my arms laid out to the side. I was very uncomfortable from getting stuck in my back with a needle to numb me for the surgery. I couldn't see anything. I could just hear talking on the other side of the curtain. It felt like forever even though the surgery takes about 45 minutes. I grew anxious as I waited to hear signs of my baby boy.

At 2:56 am my son Jaylin arrived. He was 6lbs and 8ozs. Of course, since my hands were laid out, I couldn't hold him. I had to wait   till I got in the recovery room. I couldn't believe that my baby was finally here. The baby was here but I didn't know what to do next. No one prepared me to be a mom. When the baby was inside me, I knew to be careful what I did and ate. But now I had no clue what to do. They have baby books that tell you how to care for a baby. Yes, I read some. But it just isn't the same when you are holding a screaming baby and the book doesn't have the answer.

2 Thessalonians 3:16 says "May the Lord himself, who is our source of peace, give you peace at all times and in every way. The Lord be with you all." It is very scary being a mom for the first time. I can say that I spent about 80 days out of his first year in the hospital. Jaylin was diagnosed with asthma at six months. He also had acid reflux. Despite all the hospital visits Jaylin progressed very well. He's now eight years old. I feel like I did a good job with him despite at times not knowing what I was doing. I do know that I am at peace with every decision that I make for him. I make sure that I pray before I make any decision for my children. I know that God has them covered. And that alone makes me feel so much better.

Are you a first-time mom?_____

_____

If not, how many children do you

have?_____

_____

How did you feel when you first found out you were

having your first

child?_____

_____

_____

Being a mom is an amazing role to have. Don't let anyone tell you that you aren't doing a good job. If you work all day to provide for your children, you are doing a great job. Stay at home moms we often are under appreciated. I know the feeling all too well. I applaud each and every one of you for running a household all day every day!!!

Domestic Abuse in relationships

1ˢᵗ Corinthians 13 4-8 4. Love is patient and kind; it is not jealous or conceited or proud; 5 love is not ill-mannered or selfish or irritable; love does not keep a record of wrongs; 6 love is not happy with evil but is happy with the truth. 7 Love never gives up; and its faith, hope and patience never fail. 8 Love is eternal. There are inspired messages, but they are temporary; there are gifts of speaking in strange tongues, but they will cease; there is knowledge, but it will pass.

Love can be a beautiful thing. It can also be a hurtful thing. Why would someone say they love you and hit you? Why would someone say they love you but cheat on you? I have experienced being in love and hearing the lies. Believing that there was something wrong with me, which made the other person mistreat me. But that is not the case. Hurt people hurt people. That's the bottom line. Many people don't deal with the internal issues that they have before they enter in relationships. Therefore, you have people being mentally, emotionally and physically abusive. Dealing with internal issues require a lot of acknowledgment and acceptance of pain, hurt and heartache. Many people choose to not forgive, and hold grudges their whole lives. I used to be like that. I played the victim game, blaming everyone else for the troubles in my life. It was always he did this, so I can't do better. After a while this got old. Where and when was I to become accountable for my choices and actions. Once I reached 30 years old, I had first of many aha moments. I can't dwell on what people have done to me. I needed to forgive, learn from it and move it. And that's that I have been doing for the past five years. It works for me because I no longer have anger in my heart for the men who have hurt me. I take full responsibility for everything that I allowed to happen to me.

What you are about to read is not for the faint of heart. These things did happen to me. I can't describe every grueling, heartbreaking moment. I will give you just enough so you can get the gist of what actually happened. It took me a long time to tell anyone about the abuse I suffered. I first wrote about it in an Anthology titled Please Don't Kill Me which was published in 2014. Writing for that anthology was very therapeutic for me. After that I decided I wanted to speak about it. And so, I became a member of the speaker's bureau of the organization RAINN (Rape, Abuse, Incest National Network) in 2015. Through the speaker's bureau I was able to attend several speaking events, I was featured in two documentaries, and some articles. Speaking about my situation was and still is a powerful experience for me. Through speaking I can be up close and personal with people who have or are going through the same thing. I can let them know that they will overcome their situation. It is such a joy to be the peace in someone's storm. It is simply an amazing feeling knowing that your words have touched and impacted a life.

I had never experienced domestic violence before 2004. I never saw my father hit my mom. So, when I started getting abused, I was stunned and confused. I had no idea what was happening. I knew that he was going through some things. I also knew that he was still grieving over the loss of his father. So, I used those things to justify his behavior. At first it was emotional and mental abuse. Saying things like I don't need you, No one is going to want you. Words do hurt. And when you hear the same words over and over you start to believe them. So, I believed that I wasn't good enough for anyone else. I believed that I deserved to be yelled at. It went from yelling to throwing things, to sexually assaulting me. I couldn't believe that the man I loved and lived with me treated me like an object. Could I have left? Yes. Did I leave him? Yes, several times. And I ended up going back several times. It was a roller coaster ride that made me physically sick. I lost so much weight, my hair was falling out, and I developed insomnia. To make matters worse I ended up pregnant.

I was twenty-two when I found I was pregnant for the first time. I wasn't happy at all. The situation that I was in was a complete mess. It was no way I could let a baby live through what I was going through. So, I made the decision to terminate my pregnancy. It was the most agonizing decisions of my life. I pondered on it for 4 days. The worst part of this was forgiving myself for my decision. I knew it was for the best. But it was still a struggle never the less.

Psalm 103:12 As far as the east is from the west, so far does he remove our sins from us. To this day I still think about the baby I never met. I still get in my feelings every December. It was hard but I finally forgave myself. I had to because after I terminated the pregnancy, things got worse.

Christmas 2006 I almost died. I was stabbed and punched like a punching bag. My 108-pound body was thrown around so much I blacked out several times. By the time I became fully conscious I was on my way home in a cab. My coat was ripped, my arm was bleeding and my sides hurt terribly. The cab driver offered to take me to the police station but all I wanted was my bed. I didn't go to the hospital the day of the incident. I ended up needed to go because it hurt so bad when I breathed or laughed. When I went to the ER, I told the triage people what had happened and who did it. And yet I wasn't seen for hours. I was in severe pain and just wanted to lay down. I thought a couple of Tylenols would fix the problem, so I requested to be discharged. I went home and took a couple of Tylenols. I thought my problem was solved but it wasn't. I ended up back in the ER again. This time I had an ex ray done. The ex-ray showed I had severely fractured ribs. As small in stature and weight as I was, I couldn't afford to have any fractures. The doctor prescribed oxycodone and told me to stay off my feet. Of course, that was easier said than done. I had a job. And I lived in a fifth floor walkup. Getting up and down the stairs was very difficult with fractured ribs. My ribs ended up healing, but I became addicted to the Oxycodone. I needed it to sleep. I suffered very badly from insomnia. Oxycodone for me gave me a feeling of feeling free. That's a good feeling to have when you feel like you have the weight of the world on your shoulders.

I needed the Oxy to help me cope with being stalked by my ex-boyfriend. He would call all the time, he sent a girl to my house to fight me, he threatened to hurt my family. It was a very stressful time for me. Not only was I facing what he was doing in the present moment. I was also facing what he had done to me. When people do awful, hurtful things to you, you can't just forget them. I don't understand why the saying forgive and forget exists. I will never forget what pain anyone has caused me. However, I won't let that kill my spirit or joy. I realized by harboring in the pain and hurt, I was only hurting myself. The people who caused the hurt weren't thinking about what they did to me. I had to let go. Letting go is very hard to do. I am not going to lie. It takes time and a lot of patience to get back to a space of peace. Luke 17:3-4 is the perfect reason as to why we must forgive people. It says "3. So, watch what you so! "If your brother sins, rebuke him, and if he repents, forgive him. 4. If he wins against you seven times in one day, and each time he comes to you saying, 'I repent,' you must forgive him." I learned to forgive people no matter what they do to me. Forgiveness does not make us fools. If we know someone is a liar or a thief, we can choose whether we want to continue to associate with them. So, if they continue lying or stealing from us, some point we must recognize our part in the chaos.

Some people seem to think that once you undergo a traumatic event and survive that you are ok afterward. That is so far from the truth. The effects of being in a domestic violence relationship have destroyed my self-esteem and spirit. It took me years to get to the level of confidence I have now. It's true that time heals all wounds. That and a lot of pray. I suffered for years in silence. I was isolated from people during the two-year abusive relationship. Being alone is not good for anyone. We are supposed to be around people since we are social beings. Genesis 2:18 says "Then the Lord God said, " It is not good for the man to live alone. I will make a suitable companion to help him" Notice that the bible verse said suitable companion. The companion is suitable is God's eyes not ours. Often, we are just picking and choosing people to be with and not thinking about God's input. I can honestly say if I had done this, I would have saved myself a lot of heartache.

If you are in domestic violence relationship, please get help. I know what it is like to be afraid and not know what's going to happen. If you believe in God, then trust that He has you covered. 2 Corinthians 12:9 says" but his answer was: "My grace is all you need, for my power is greatest when you are weak. "I am most happy, then. To be proud of my weaknesses, in order to feel the protection of Christ's power over me." You can and you will overcome your situation. Let my testimony be proof that God is amazing, and his words are the truth.

Marriage and Infidelity

Proverbs 6:32- But a man who commits adultery doesn't have any sense. He is just destroying himself

I don't know why people cheat when in relationships. I wish there was a way to tell who cheaters are so I could avoid them. I think cheating is a disgusting choice that has devastating consequences for many people. People don't think when they cheat about their partner, children, and other family members. They don't think about the consequences of their actions. I have heard people say cheating is a mistake. Where is the mistake? How could a person not know that they are with someone else that isn't their partner? It just doesn't make any sense to me at all. I experienced this too many times in my life. I know some of the times came from me not knowing any better. I didn't grow up with my father at home. I had no idea what loved was or what it looked like. I think what was very detrimental to my relationships were the words "I love you" My father would always tell me that but never did anything to show me. As I got older, I just accepted the words with no actions. But until I learned that love is a verb, that requires some type of action, I was a target for cheating men.

Having a boyfriend is one thing, having a husband is a whole different ball game. I hold my husband to a higher standard than any man I simply dated. Why? The Bible says in *Mark 10:6-9 6 "But in the beginning, at the time of creation, 'God made them male and female,' as the scripture says, 7 and for this reason a man will leave his father and mother and unite with his wife, 8 and the two will become one' So they are no longer two, but one. 9 No human being must separate, then, what God has joined together."* Marriage is sacred. We should all know and understand that. Unfortunately, some people have no regard for God's word. No regard for the marriage itself. It's all about their wants and needs. It's a sad situation that I found myself in as both a wife and other woman. Twice in my life I found out I was dating a married man. I honestly didn't know. When you meet someone, you tend to want to give them the benefit of the doubt. Some people are just that good at lying. They hide the fact that they have children and a wife. As sad as it is many people get caught up in situations that they aren't aware of all the details.

Both times it happened to me there were no indications of a wife. When a person makes you feel like you are the only one in their life, why should you think otherwise. It wasn't until I got the call from the wife did, I realize that I had been played. I instantly knew that I was done with the relationships. The wives didn't have to tell me anything. But they choose to take their anger out on me as if I was the one to blame.

I am a firm believer in Karma. Although I didn't know about the marriages of the men I was involved with, I knew that I was going to feel what the wives felt at one point in my life.

I got married the first time on Valentine's Day of 2012. The karma I got hit me fast and hard. I didn't expect it so soon after getting married. The only difference with me was that I did not go back and forth with the other person. Some women knew and didn't care. Others were innocent parties in a game my ex-husband was playing. Either way I wasn't the one to blame the woman. I took responsibility for my part in being married to a cheater. And when I signed my divorce papers, I didn't have no regrets. I didn't shed a tear or put up a fight. I was tired of the pure disrespect of the man I married. I was tired of the lies, and constant traffic of women he was messing around with. It became overwhelming and draining to be married to someone who thought cheating was a game. Unfortunately, it took me longer than I wanted to get a divorce. I knew that I was done with him, but I struggled with what God would think of me. *Mark 10:12 says "In the same way a woman who divorces her husband and marries another man commits adultery"* It was a hard-internal struggle to endure. But I knew that I couldn't take much more of being sad and miserable. Something had to give.

At some point when people betray you, you want to hear why for closure. I wanted closure so that I could walk away from this marriage and not feel bad. When I was told that there were over seventy women involved, I nearly lost my mind. Then to top it off this occurred before and during our marriage. I was most hurt because I asked him the night before we got married if he cheated at any time. Of course, he said no. But it was all a lie. I no longer need to hear anything else. My mind was made up. In 2015 I filed for divorce from my ex-husband. It hurt in the beginning because of course I was in love, but I quickly got over it. I remarried on November 1st, 2016. I never wanted to experience marriage again. They say never say never right.

This time I am content in my marriage. Marriage is hard work. The work should be done between two willing parties. One person can't fight to make a marriage work.

So, for all those people out there who think no one would want them after a breakup, don't believe that. You never know what's in store for you. God has the final say in all aspects of our lives.

Time to get to work

Ephesians 1:9- God did what he had purposed and made known to us the secret plan he had already decided to complete by means of Christ.

Many are chosen but few are called. It doesn't matter if you are qualified to do something. If God sends the call to you, just answer it. We will never know everything there is to know to do things. When I first published a book, all I knew how to do was write. I learned and studied the entire writing process. Now I teach it to others. So many people let fear, and other people stop them from living their best life. You can't live your best life if you are living for others. Yes, we must make decisions and choices for our families but that doesn't mean that we give up our dreams. I struggled with this for a while. I know the feeling of doing everything else but what I wanted to do. I decided in 2018 that I wasn't going to live my life for others. It's not easy. You must find a balance between work, family and your dreams. But you can do it. As 2019 approaches I am going into the new year with a clear vision. You need to have clarity in order to move forward with an idea, dream, or pretty much anything you want to do. If you don't have clarity, you are going to be doing everything else but what you need to be doing.

The struggles and things I went through aren't all detailed in this book. Yes, I went through a lot more than this. I decided to break this book up into three parts. One dedicated to each of my children. My son Jaylin is my first born. He has helped shape me into the person I am today.

I have a special needs disabled child named Jayshaun. He has taught me the importance of patience. I struggled with patience for so many years of my life.

My last son is Jayson. He was born at twenty-nine weeks (Seven months) Having a premature baby in the NICU is a very devastating experience.

Contact Me

I look forward to you reading the rest of the series. I hoped that you enjoyed this book. Feel free follow me on social media

Instagram @Sheri_N_Simmons

Facebook Sheri Simmons

Email me at Sherisimmons729@gmail.com

Divine Assignment

www.ingramcontent.com/pod-product-compliance
Lightning Source LLC
Chambersburg PA
CBHW032053040426
42449CB00007B/1095